The Celibate Seeker:

An Exploration of Celibacy as a Modern Spiritual Practice

TAT Foundation Press

Wheeling, WV

Main entry under title: The Celibate Seeker

1. Spirituality   2. Philosophy

Library of Congress Control Number: 2009931575

ISBN: 978-0-9799630-3-2

Published by TAT Foundation Press

Visit our website: www.tatfoundation.org

The unmarried is anxious about the things of the Lord, how he may please the Lord; but the married man is anxious about worldly matters, how he may please his wife. And he is drawn in diverging directions—his interests are divided, and he is distracted. — Paul in 1 Corinthians 7 (verses 32-34)

To put a cork in Old Faithful is as ill fated as it is dangerous. — Anonymous

What do you hope sex will accomplish for you? — Richard Rose

Contents

Introduction

Celibacy as a spiritual practice is generally considered the purview of religious orders and an esoteric discipline whose origin and purpose is foggy at best. Much of the discussion regarding celibacy involves derision and disbelief. The derision is typically aimed at the Roman Catholic Church whose 800-year-old insistence upon a celibate priesthood is often seen as the catalyst for perversion and abuse. The Hindu and Buddhist traditions of celibate monks and nuns, perhaps because of their more exotic flavor and rarity in this country, attract far less criticism. The disbelief arises from puzzlement over why anyone would want to be celibate and doubt that, even with a compelling reason, one would have the will power to keep the commitment.

Suffice it to say that over the last few thousand years and for numerous reasons, countless men and women have chosen celibacy for at least part of their lives. The exploration of this historical background and the cultural context of celibacy is best left to such authoritative works as Elizabeth Abbott's 496-page *A History of Celibacy.*[1] I present a much narrower slice (and fewer pages) of the celibate life: the practical benefits of a period of celibacy for those on a spiritual path.

Referring to the highly individual nature of spiritual practice, the teacher Richard Rose used to quote an old farmer's saying, "There are many paths to the top of the hill." My particular spiritual path began with misery and despair. Misery brought about by a foiled romantic ambition named Ann, and despair by a meaningless graduate research program investigating nitrogen losses from agricultural soil. This depressing pair of emotions circled my first year of graduate school like buzzards attracted to the corpse of failed dreams.

Into my misery and despair came the work of Richard Rose and his students. The emptiness became at once amplified and filled by the spiritual quest—the tantalizing possibility of devoting one's life to the pursuit of an answer to the feeling that something was missing in life. That pursuit had an end goal—enlightenment, Samadhi, realization, the Absolute—and that end goal left the finder for all time satisfied.

Richard Rose left me haunted by the feeling there was *something* to me other than being another link in the endless chain of life and death. The man exuded profundity like cold air from a cave. He extolled a workman-like attitude regarding this quest for ultimate Truth, best summed up by the adage "backing away from untruth." By continually rejecting what is less true about our self, we eventually discover what is true.

After a second half-hearted year of graduate school, I left and eventually spent three years living on Mr. Rose's farm. I spent the bulk of my time reading, meditating, and talking with others interested in spiritual matters. Living in the country, there weren't a lot of distractions, and I tried to focus on observing the mind and discovering the source of thought.

Every couple of weeks or so, as my inspiration faded and I doubted my ability to find an answer, I would visit Mr. Rose. In those visits, I probably heard him say "be celibate" more than any other piece of advice. So much so, that I would occasionally remind him, "but Mr. Rose, I *am* being celibate," in hopes of hearing what else I should be doing. Yet, he was reluctant to give advice beyond a few points he considered critical. Why did Mr. Rose see celibacy as a cornerstone of spiritual success?

Success is proportional to energy applied to an endeavor. This holds true whether you are climbing Mount Everest, seeking a spiritual realization, or growing potatoes. A tremendous amount of our energy is spent trying to get sexual partners, having sex, and managing the myriad aftereffects of sex. If we redirected the energy devoted to sex to another pursuit, that pursuit would benefit. Rose wrote:

> Individual genius, is directly related to the
> ability by that individual to know and store, and
> properly use that quantum-energy. Likewise
> with spiritual progress. Spiritual progress
> depends upon that transmuted energy.[2]

Mr. Rose believed a person possessed a quantity (quantum) of energy they could generate, store, and use for a higher purpose. For example, your body converts food from a meal into energy and you walk down to the bar and party all evening. Or you use the energy from that meal to study a book or practice meditation—same energy, but two different results. The idea of using our energy wisely makes perfect sense, but few exert a conscious effort to manage their energy. Beyond the physical level, Rose also pointed to energy used to propel one into a Universal or Pure-Mind dimension.[3]

Almost all of what Mr. Rose wrote regarding celibacy is in his book *Energy Transmutation, Between-ness and Transmission* (often called the Transmission Papers). He wrote little on the topic and said even less in his public lectures. Yet in private, it was a frequent topic. In the Transmission Papers, he gives one likely reason:

> This paper cannot advise all individually about
> each individual approach to energy building
> through celibacy, because all men are constructed
> differently or at least have developed sex habits
> of varying intensities and types of sexual action.
> Fetishes, associations, particular inhibitions, plus
> a wide variety of subtle incidental factors must
> be taken into account with each individual case
> when giving advice.[4]

To focus energy on one goal made sense to me as a way to increase the odds of success. Like television, sex was a distraction, though much more powerful. In addition to focusing our energy, Mr. Rose felt celibacy increased one's intuition. There were also stories that harkened to those of the Muscular Christianity movement: that celibacy increased one's physical stamina, would increase one's ability to tolerate cold, and help stave off illness. I recall the story of two or three people who walked barefoot through the snow to test their celibate strength. One of them got frostbite, "because he wasn't really celibate," so the story went.

Celibacy means no sex and no masturbation. I think that is an all inclusive list of sexual expression, but who knows what a desperate imagination will think of. Speaking of imagination, Mr. Rose considered daydreaming about sex while practicing celibacy a sure route to various physical ills—such as prostatitis and prostate cancer. Celibacy was to be physical and mental. Tantric practices of sex without orgasm were not as well known in Mr. Rose's day as now. I am certain they would not be considered a celibate practice.

Rose often recommended people try celibacy for a month. Read *The Albigen Papers* before you begin, he would say, then read it after a month of celibacy. Your understanding will be deeper after being celibate. It's a good test and worth your time to try. What's to lose?

As explained in the Transmission Papers, Rose advised celibacy as part of an all-out assault on the truth occurring during our twenties and thirties. Celibacy past the age of forty was considered a dubious affair as he felt the body lost its "elasticity" and prostate troubles were sure to arise. However, I have talked with a few over-forty celibates who testify to no ill effects.

"The aim should be temporary, total abstinence from the conscious sex act.... By 'temporary' is meant the number of years that are needed to reach our goal."[5] Yet to simply be celibate and imagine one is continually adding to a spiritual bank account is not enough. Celibacy is one tool for the spiritual quest. The energy saved has to be transmuted through action along several lines of work which Rose called the three-fold path.[6]

I found celibacy and the spiritual quest of benefit beyond imagination. Yet the testimony of one or two people is a tiny data set. What follows, is the collective wisdom of several people who tried the celibacy experiment within the context of a spiritual search. Each was sent a set of questions to help guide their reflections on the experience. The questions were:

1. Did celibacy increase your energy?
2. Did celibacy increase your intuition?
3. What other benefits did you derive from celibacy?
4. Why did you stop being celibate (if you have stopped)?
5. What advice would you give someone trying celibacy? Things to watch out for, ways to help success, etc.
6. Any other message-in-a-bottle thoughts you would leave with people?

The rest of this book will proceed, more or less, down this line of questions allowing us to compare the experiences of several people.

Chapter I
Celibacy and Energy

You've gotta conserve your sex energy in order to do your work. It's the same energy. When I started to write or did a picture, I stopped all my sex activities. Sex divides your mind. – Mae West

Seinfeld, a popular television comedy from the 1990s, featured an episode on celibacy. George is forced to go without sex when his girlfriend thinks she has mononucleosis. Within a few days, George's memory and concentration improve dramatically. He learns Portuguese, studies chaos theory, teaches Yankees baseball players how to improve their batting, and builds science experiments for the local school—all because, as his friend Jerry theorizes, most of his brain has always thought about sex. With his mind clear, he can now focus. I wonder what the genesis for the script was. Did the writer have an intuition about celibacy's effects?

Despite conflicting scientific evidence,[7,8] celibacy is a common practice in sports such as boxing, traditional Indian wrestling, soccer, and weight-lifting.[9] "It gives you a little more quickness, better reflexes and more of an edge. You don't want to give up your energies before you go to war," said former undisputed heavyweight boxing champ Lennox Lewis.[10] Tibetan monks are known to develop amazing physical abilities such as drying ice-cold sheets with the heat from their bodies (tummo).[11] In the realm of mental energy, Jacob Needleman credits the creative energy of the Shaker community to the "authentic sublimation of sexual energy."[12]

From the mental to the physical, what did our survey respondents notice about their energy during their celibacy? Did it increase their energy?

Mr. A: Celibacy did not increase my energy but it clarified it; I noticed that my energy, like a strong wind that blows a weathervane from different directions, just blew from one direction while I was celibate. My energies were more unified, like polarized light—all going in one direction like a continual wind. My energy was more constant.

Mr. B: Absolutely yes, both mental and physical, but with some ebb and flow. At times the energy increase would seem like I was riding a roller coaster (more physical); at times, periods of calm and peace, physically and mentally, followed by periods of increasing irritation; at times anger; at times lethargy.

Mr. C: In the years that I was celibate, I did not experience any greater level of physical, psychological, or psychic energy. I wasn't capable of greater feats of any kind because of it. I couldn't withstand cold any better, or physical privations any better, or tune into other people any more. If I broke with celibacy I certainly felt the temporary loss of physical and psychic energy... I think most any male is well aware of that. But I didn't think I was "dialing heaven," as Rose would say, just because I was remaining celibate.

Mr. D: Whether or not celibacy increased my energy is a matter of semantics, possibly. However, celibacy definitely increases my ability to channel any energy I do have at the time, and on occasion to access a greater reservoir of energy that exists elsewhere, seemingly. It is my belief that an adroit mind can access all the energy in the Universe, or at least all the energy in a cubic centimeter of space, which may prove to be identical in the final analysis. A sound body helps, as well as a balanced neutral mind backed by a determined unwavering commitment and force of will. It could be compared to focusing a laser, which demands that all available photons be summoned to a line or point.

Mr. E: I don't notice an increase in energy with being celibate. However, when I once had a "hiccup" [break in celibacy], for several days after it was as if I had the flu, I was so tired. So it seems there has been a dramatic change but I have not noticed it because it has been gradual. I never noticed drops in energy with dissipation before being celibate, but now my mind feels foggier even for maybe a day and a half after a wet dream.

Mr. F: I definitely had more energy while being celibate.

Mr. G: I could not say that celibacy increased my energy.

Mr. H: I find an increase in energy when celibate, and it can be used for whatever. I knew bike racers who were celibate because they found an increase in energy.

Mr. I: I have drawn the personal conclusion that celibacy is a huge boon in terms of energy, but that energy boon is much more mental than it is physical. However, I would still say that there is a physical effect. I would not set out to prove that effect to an empirical scientist, but I have noticed specifically a weakening of the legs while not being celibate.

In terms of the mental energy, I think that celibacy is a huge help in terms of increasing my ability to focus on a given task. I notice that I generally have more attention and interest in the world around me than I used to, and that interest can maintain itself for longer periods of time than it once could. One of the most noticeable effects of celibacy is while reading things, the words sink deeper while I am celibate.

Mr. J: It did not make me Superman. It did not keep me from getting ill (e.g., common cold, flu, etc.). And I was still tired after a hard day's work. I do not recall a tremendous change in physical or mental energy levels, either after initiating the celibacy or subsequent to cessation later in life. But I must qualify my situation by stating that I have always tempered my sexual outlets, even during my teenage years. If I were to speculate, someone who is quite active in a sexual sense may experience marked contrasts in energy levels as a result of celibacy.

Mr. K: Yes, it did.

Mr. L: Yes. It appears to develop to a plateau typically in the twenty-one day range, but actually continues to build more subtly.

Mr. M: I did not notice an increase in my physical or mental energy. Although it did not increase my mental energy, it did improve my focus by removing a major distraction.

Mr. N: I wasn't much sensitive to energy changes. I attribute that to a slow metabolism, with mood-changes and body-speed generally on the slow side. I became celibate after receiving perhaps the first clearly intuitive message as an adult. It happened as if a light bulb went on in my head, and the words that formed were: "My only chance for mental clarity is through a prolonged period of celibacy."

One of the startling changes—really the only one I think I can honestly tie to my celibacy—had to do with a physical change. I'd done a lot of ice-skating in the winters as a kid, but I'd always had trouble with weak ankles. After about a year of celibacy, I went ice-skating with my wife—something I'd only done on rare occasions as an adult, but always with the same ankle problem. But this time there was absolutely no wobble in my ankles.

I thought at the time, and still think, that it was an example of cosmic humor. I had considered myself weak-ankled in the sense of weak-kneed, meaning lacking in courage, or resolution. The resolution to become celibate was a mental resolution, and it undoubtedly had at least one physical repercussion.

Mr. O: I have only experimented with celibacy for a short period of time, but there has been a clear boost of energy. It was most obvious to me one time when breaking the celibacy. It felt like an internal engine was turned off and that my internal drive left me. Another thing I have noticed is how much time and energy one can waste on sex. Not that it is a bad thing, unless you are trying to conserve energy for something more important to you (ex. success in sports, business, or a spiritual pursuit).

Mr. P: Yes, absolutely. But what does that mean? It meant I had an ability to concentrate and maintain a focus of attention noticeably beyond what I had previously experienced and beyond those I observed in my daily routines. I was frequently astounded at how often—in a business setting—executives to whom I was demonstrating management system software could not keep their eyes open during demonstrations taking place in the morning hours! They seemed to lack the mental energy to focus.

Over half the respondents found some form of increased energy while celibate. Mr. J's speculation regarding the increase in energy being proportional to the level of prior sexual activity seems sensible. Those who derive the most energetic benefit, however, tend to have the greatest difficulty maintaining their celibacy. My experience is in line with those who noticed an increased ability to focus.

Chapter II
Celibacy and Intuition

Celibacy develops creative genius and intuition—items needed to carry a man where there are no railroad tracks. – Richard Rose in Rose Quotes and Notes: 1986-1993

By way of heredity and training, I am blessed and cursed with a logical mind. The recognition that intuition was a way of obtaining information and making decisions was a revelation to me.

That celibacy would result in a clearer mind, more capable of hearing the sometimes quiet ring of intuition may have a thread of scientific support. Though I found no studies of long-term celibacy in healthy individuals, "After three months without sex, which is not so uncommon for some athletes, testosterone dramatically drops to levels close to children's levels," says professor of endocrinology Emmanuele A. Jannini.[13] This is a tantalizing statement considering Jesus' admonition to "welcome the kingdom of God as a little child."[14]

The belief that we were more intuitive as children is not uncommon.[15] Proof of that, or even a valid method of measuring intuition is more uncertain. One interesting study found that pre-school and kindergarten children out-performed third through six-graders predicting the flight of a ball from a curved tube. The youngest children performed at the same level as college-age students![16]

Perhaps someday more in-depth studies will lend increased support to a connection between celibacy and intuition or childhood and intuition. Until then, let us see what the subjective observations of our respondents reveal. Does celibacy increase your intuition?

Mr. A: While I was celibate, I was wholly concentrated on my inner world and workings. I was fully engaged in trying to understand myself in all my various actions and reactions. I was trying to understand all the things that motivated me. I tried to understand my promptings and urges, where they were coming from and why.

When I became celibate and committed myself to being celibate, the earlier mentioned increased stabilizing of my personal perceived energy levels was also mirrored by a more stable personality platform; like looking through binoculars at distant objects on the solid stone of a lookout as opposed to hovering in a helicopter with binoculars to my eyes trying to pick out subtle details in a whole scene jumping with the vibration of the hovering machine.

I think I became more aware of, accustomed to and attuned to the still small voice that accompanies many whisperings of what is commonly referred to as intuition. I could hear it; I could notice it. Before, I was too buffeted to do much along those lines.

Mr. B: Absolutely. There were times that I got the feeling that I could read people's thoughts if I looked at them, or could pick up their actual thoughts, but not by trying to do so, it would just happen. Also, the internal dialogue in my head was getting a flow of thoughts that increased thinking about thinking without my trying to do so. In the same vein, it seemed that I had increasing thoughts coming into my head, so to speak, about the working of my head, and that I "understood" Rose's Psychology of the Observer[17] analysis of the working of the mind, and that in every situation with people, there was a more acute sensitivity concerning what they were really thinking and what they were actually saying when they spoke, and some greater degree of understanding their personal plight.

Mr. D: It is difficult to assess whether or not celibacy increases one's intuition. I believe celibacy allows the dust to fall from the lens, so to speak, and in that manner, may facilitate one's ability to quickly assess situations, and understand concepts and the true nature of things.

Mr. E: I can't say for sure it increased my intuition although I did notice when I had read *The Albigen Papers* the first time, when I was not being celibate, I had not been able to get much of anything out of it, however when reading it the second time, after having been celibate for three months, I was amazed how much content was in the book. I saw the same thing happen with the *Energy Transmutation* [*Between-ness and Transmission*] *Papers*, where after having been celibate for a few months I was able to understand what the point of some of the lines were, whereas before it was like the whole thing went over my head. With these books, though, I don't know how much had to do with being celibate and how much had to do with having been exposed to... spiritual thinking longer, or my mind clearing up some from confrontation.[18]

Mr. F: During the peaceful times my mind was quieter and this helped with intuition.

Mr. G: Intuition was increased to the extent that: I can hold myself without any "remonstrating with myself" as Rose would say. In other words, with not having anything to hide my head is clearer, simpler from a psychological standpoint.

Mr. H: I am beginning to think that celibacy doesn't increase intuition as much as it makes it easier to hear, and to act on.

Mr. I: This is not so clear to me, since I do very little to try to validate my intuition. However, what I have noticed is that I am more sensitive around others while I am celibate, but paradoxically, I am also less likely to get caught up in their story, perhaps because I don't feel the need to atone for repressed shame and guilt. I feel more while celibate, but as I said, I do not go out of my way to validate those feelings.

Mr. J: Unequivocally—yes. But here again, I was "sensitive" from the outset. The odd part of the story is that I didn't know I was sensitive until Richard Rose pointed it out to me sometime in 1986 or 1987. During celibacy, I became acutely aware of the possibility that I may be picking up other peoples' thoughts. More importantly, over the years, the celibacy improved clarity and focus, and it became much more apparent to me that I was engaged in spiritual activities that were truly nonsensical. In the words of Rose, I was better able to "back away from untruth" by seeing thought patterns and activities that were not expediting my attempts at self-definition. Lest the reader becomes overly enthralled with the possibilities of riding a "high horse" of celibate superiority, I do not know if engaging in celibacy will improve intuition for everyone. But I believe the odds are quite in favor of the mind's improved capacity to intuit and reason during celibacy.

Mr. K: Yes, very much so. I have noticed an increased ability to understand or see something without logically arriving at an answer through brute force. The idea or understanding seems to more easily come loose and arrive in my awareness. It's not that I have new and overwhelming hunches on which stocks to pick, but just an overall feeling of ease when confronted with a problem because a solution seems to appear via intuition rather than just linear thinking. Maybe it's really a combination of both, increased intuition and increased clarity of thinking.

Mr. L: Yes. The intuition improves, and sensitivity to subtle impressions. Increasingly more subtle sensitivity manifests as time passes. The ability to pick up on others' thoughts manifests more frequently.

Mr. M: Yes. My intuitive insights usually come when I'm very focused on the problem. Celibacy improved my focus.

Mr. N: I don't know if celibacy increased my intuition. I know that my mind had no argument with it (which was astounding to me).

Mr. O: My intuition has increased in the period I have experimented with celibacy, but I don't know if it is because of the celibacy. Many things in my life have changed in that period and just being aware of what intution is and how it works could also be the cause.

Mr. P: Yes. I believe intuitive function requires a consistent mental and emotional reference point. Intense experience is jarring to the mental reference point—and sexual experience also affects the emotional reference point because emotions are so closely tied to the physical state of the body. The sexual roller coaster that nearly everyone rides vacillates between anger and empathy. The shifting point of reference which is not itself observed, leads to inconsistent evaluations of our world experience, let alone our attempts to evaluate our reaction to that experience.

Nearly every respondent felt celibacy played some role in either improving intuition or their ability to perceive and act on intuitions. I relate most to Mr. A's idea of the stable platform celibacy provides and the lessoning of the buffeting urges of the mind. Typically, our only respite from these urges is in what Mr. Rose called the "five minutes of sanity" that occur after the sexual act. "We may momentarily have the freedom from lust, a respite occasionally in which we see the absurdity of the frenzy of a few minutes past…. This is the time when we should not run and hide, or eat, but sit and think."[19] The desire is satiated and the thoughts prompted by it die away. Imagine if you had that sanity all the time….

Chapter III
Other Benefits of Celibacy

If warriors want to have enough energy to see, they must become misers with their sexual energy. – don Juan in Carlos Castaneda's The Fire from Within

While Richard Rose emphasized the energetic and intuitive benefits of celibacy, our physical and mental idiosyncrasies ensure that a practice as radical as celibacy will have other effects. What other benefits did people derive from celibacy?

❈

Mr. A: I happened onto new understandings about myself, inner-felt promptings, intention, volition and accomplishment of pursued goals. I realized for myself the utter necessity to will consciously that my 'energy' salvaged from and related to inhibited sexual activity be sent in a definite direction. I saw that my body was a thing apart from the "me" that notices things about my behavior. I'd be moving towards, literally, activity to release built up energy tension and then "wake up" in time to say no. This would go on while awake but not always paying attention or aware. I saw the insidious nature of a pressure cooker looking for its own outlet of pressure.

Mr. B: Greater understanding of my own personal plight.

Mr. C: I don't think God or any other Powers That Be have any greater regard for the celibate person per se. There is nothing spiritual in itself about abstaining from sex. There *is* value in abstaining from sex for an explicitly spiritual purpose. The sacrifice immediately puts one at odds with one's body and the

22

rest of society, and makes one excruciatingly aware of their position. It is almost impossible to live within our society and be celibate without asking, every day, "Why the hell am I doing this?" That psychological pressure is certainly a strong motivator to make the most of your spiritual vector.

I also believe that sexual motivation can cloud people's judgment. If you spend most of your time "thinking with your dick," as... would say, then you are habitually in a frame of mind that is mundane at best, predatory at worst, and primarily self-involved. If one engages in promiscuous sex, one increasingly becomes emotionally calloused and "shut down," primarily to avoid confronting the ever-more dastardly nature of one's character. Being celibate, or at least being chaste (either completely celibate or in a committed, long-term, stable marriage) can spare one that psychic damage. I think Rose himself was aware that celibacy was more a means of "damage control," of maintaining original purity rather than attaining a super-human potential; he often spoke about celibacy as a means of "returning to innocence," which for him was synonymous with "emerging from self-obsession."

I also think that celibacy is a powerful means to affirming one's own sense of control. Rose said, "A man that jacks off doesn't respect himself." If a person can abstain from sex, they can probably exercise self-control in almost any other line of human endeavor. The level of psychological self-awareness and control (i.e. "turning the inner head away") required by true celibacy can only be helpful to a spiritual search. It is especially powerful just in terms of freeing the mind from perpetual obsession with reverie and giving it the means to focus on something more meaningful.

Which brings us to... celibacy as a practical matter. I think this is the best reason and most often missed reason. Simply put, sex (in any form, however subtle or inhibited) inevitably leads to relationships, which lead to marriages, which lead to children, which lead to mortgages, careers, commitments, and the complete loss of a personal life. I don't think marriage had any significant impact on my spiritual life, in either a physical or a metaphysical sense, but having children changed absolutely <u>everything</u>. If you believe that having a strong spiritual life requires a tremendous commitment of time, energy, and thought, then having children is probably not a good idea. (There are, as it turns out, tremendous opportunities for spiritual growth in being a parent; however, those benefits do not outweigh the level of freedom one loses in having a family.)

Mr. D: One of the first benefits to celibacy, at least for me, which has been corroborated by others, including Mr. Rose, is a certain sense of "freedom" that is difficult to describe unless one experiences it. This is more a psychological sense of well-being, perhaps, although it definitely includes an ability to "ponder the moment" a bit longer, before falling into a decision, which may later prove to be a habit. Not that celibacy is a cure-all for psychological engrams,[20] but rather that it allows us "a break from Nature" as Mr. Rose often wrote and said. A break from Nature is what we need, if we want to think clearly. This last statement is a postulation until proven by the individual. I have found it to be true.

Mr. E: I have noticed overall my internal state is less turbulent since I started trying to be celibate, although I am not sure how much of that has do with celibacy and how much with confrontation and meditation. Also, I think it was easier later to find the discipline to develop a regular meditation practice because I knew I had been successful with a hard commitment.

Mr. F: It is interesting to observe whole worlds of ultimately illusory thinking that are built up from the sex drive. If some of this thinking is caught early enough and not followed, some suffering can be avoided.

Mr. H: One of the other main things it brings is a stability or peace of mind. It makes work and related stresses much easier to handle…. I think the accumulated effect of effort must add up, because I notice a long term, steady effect of greater well-being and productivity, compassion, insight, etc.

Another noticeable effect is the diminishing of negative emotions, which helps restore energy in itself. These 'dark moods' used to lead into sex much more frequently. Now, it's easier to ride them out, and the severity is less.

Mr. I: Self respect is perhaps the biggest benefit I have received from the celibate periods in my life. The absence of wasting my sexual energy, and not having my mind run by lust has resulted in greater personal confidence.

Mr. J: On the most mundane level, total abstention will disengage a seeker from distractions connected with sexual relationships. Likewise, celibacy will inhibit pursuits that grow out of odd sexual practices. The key is gaining any possible edge during a spiritual search. Celibacy helps a seeker to stay sharp and focused on a goal (Enlightenment) that the body and mind seemingly resist at all costs.

Mr. K: Much increased clarity of mind, reduction in irritability overall. However, I have noticed that in the first couple of weeks of celibacy an increase in anger or unprovoked rage episodes. I suspect this might be due to a damming of energy that isn't transmuted. After a few weeks of celibacy this seems to taper off. So, while my overall countenance has seemed to have softened and the frequency of angry episodes seems to have come down, the amplitude of the peaks appears to increase shortly after celibacy is initiated.

The increased ability to think clearly and solve problems by way of lateral thinking is the most evident for me. I feel like I have "great" ideas more often that solve problems better than before. This can be at work, or in my personal and spiritual life.

Mr. L: Freedom from distraction resulting in greater clarity of thinking. Increased ability to focus and engage in prolonged reading and meditation.

Mr. M: Fewer negative feelings, less craving, better focus.

Mr. N: Celibacy initially descended on me like a gift from heaven, and it lasted nearly five years without any struggle on my part. I assume it was a cosmic gift that was necessary for my path—like a hypnotic suggestion that gives the body a break from a nicotine addiction. After that initial five years, it took me almost six years to regain celibacy for more than a few months at a time. I have a feeling that when prolonged celibacy returned, it was a result of the struggle, and I feel that the struggle gave me whatever insight I have into what Rose called between-ness.[21]

Mr. O: Less mental noise. It seems that my mind is responding to what I experience and when I am sexually active, sex related thoughts occur with a higher frequency. Again, not a bad thing, but it takes attention away from other things.

Mr. P: It gave me a mental and emotional consistency that was pivotal in seeing more clearly and objectively, free from the roller coaster of mood swings, and providing some detachment from those experiences, beginning with adolescence, that so challenge the developing sense of an adult self.

Mr. Q: I think celibacy is a prime contributor towards factor X. Factor X—that element of grace with which I seemed doomed to fail without. I can't explain it—well, I can but I don't feel like it—my energy dispensed sexually somehow seems to come back and hit me in the head like a boomerang that I've thrown and forgotten about. You reap what you sow they say. Celibacy seems to be a way of controlling what you sow.

Clarity, stability, strength of mind and purpose—it is difficult to find one word to summarize these varying experiences. I'm reminded of the admonition the great mystic Douglas Harding made to a friend—Simplify! To me, celibacy simplifies the exterior and interior life, and from that arises many benefits.

Chapter IV

To Stop or to Carry On

*Homer Simpson: Hey, is it true that you priest guys can't ever…
er… y'know?*
*Priest: Well, I have to admit that the vow of celibacy is one of
our sterner challenges.*
*Homer: Celibacy! I was talking about the meat on Friday thing!
Man! You guys have more crazy rules than Blockbuster video….*

I once made a vow not to eat donuts until I achieved enlightenment… I know it sounds ludicrous, but it was a serious decision made after long deliberation. Some years later, I decided that the vow achieved its purpose and I could eat a donut even though I wasn't enlightened. That, too, was a difficult decision.

Following, we will hear from people just beginning the practice and those with years of experience. What are the reasons that people stop or struggle with being celibate?

Mr. A: I think I stopped being celibate because my time to do it was done.

I let the object drop to the ground, this celibacy that I had carried faithfully with me wherever I went for four years or so, one day that I remember as vividly as though I was still right there, in Switzerland where I happened to be.

I was faced or confronted with a decision. My decision meant betraying my faithfulness to my celibate lifestyle. It felt like a betrayal. The time was over. I see that in retrospect and felt, when I dropped that object, that I was leaving a chapter of my life behind forever. I was.

Mr. B: Why did I stop? Entities[22] had my number and called it in.

I drifted too long on a plateau, so to speak, met..., and allowed myself to get involved with her emotionally. She flattered me, I didn't resist and continue on my path, but succumbed; presto-chango equals kids. During separation and divorce, I went another extended period of about eight months, but did not have the same results as earlier.

Mr. C: I got married. Once you're married, sex is by and large a positive element. It is a force of gravitation that naturally binds the couple together and fosters genuine intimacy. Like I said, I see chastity as more important than celibacy.

Why did I get married? Frankly, I lost faith in celibacy as a necessary element of the spiritual path. I believed I had a greater chance of being happy by being married. And I was right; by and large, I <u>am</u> happier. But it cost me a tremendous amount of spiritual drive, and I am still haunted by the fear that I have paid too high a price for that relative happiness.

Mr. D: I have been celibate for mostly one-year periods, with occasional periods of one-and-one-half years. There were also many periods of celibacy that lasted for six or nine months. I was either unable, due to my particular constitution, or unwilling, to remain celibate for any longer periods. Also, to this day, my life shows a continuation of this pattern, with usually six to nine months in the cycle—sometimes less.

Mr. E: I still am being celibate, and it has been six and a half months since I had a "hiccup." What I noticed when I had the slip up back then, was that for a few days before the event, I had stopped turning my internal head away from sexual reverie, and it built and increased until I couldn't turn my head away from it. Since then, I've been trying to be more careful not to act on reasons to temporarily stop turning my head away from those thoughts.

Mr. F: I've never had much long term success with celibacy which is one of the main reasons I left the spiritual life. This lack of character has caused much sadness for me over the years.... I guess it just means I'm not serious about seeking, but I would like to become more serious.

My periods of celibacy have been times of greater peace and greater turmoil. It can be very peaceful to take a vacation from nature's games for a bit, but the force of the dance of life seems to come back even stronger after those times of peace. I can clearly see the grasping and pain that the sex drive causes, but I find the pull irresistible at times.

Mr. H: I've also noticed there is an 'X' factor, or Grace, involved. When I've had the greatest success, there was something there protecting me from the attacks, helping stop the cycle, including wet dreams. Then, for some unknown reason, as yet, it goes away—which is when I realize it was there. I think this could be an anterior self that is convinced about one way or the other.

I quit being celibate awhile back, getting married and all. One thing I've noticed is that getting older makes the body a lot less pliable. Wet dreams went away years ago, and thankfully the drive has lessened as well. I don't think I could get away with a long period of celibacy now, not in terms of months into years. I can say that many of the effects of celibacy continue, such as hearing the intuition, and not worrying as much, but maybe that's just aging. This lends credence to the advice that celibacy should be done while relatively young.

Mr. I: I have not stopped being celibate, but those periods of time when I have failed to be celibate have come from a lack of clarity about desires and also not knowing what I was doing very well. I have learned to turn my head away from sexual thinking better than I could in the past, and that ability has resulted in an increased ability to remain celibate. Temptation, though, is always an issue, and never to be dismissed as having been completely conquered.

Mr. J: At the age of about 31, I broke my celibacy because I was floating adrift in the spiritual doldrums, feeling like I was no longer destined to discover my Source.

Mr. K: Maximum celibacy to date has been seven weeks this go-around. The bottom line is that an image is formed in the mind and acted upon. Once the image is formed it is almost too late. I guess becoming celibate is learning how to avoid indulging in and forming the mental imagery. But above all, there has to be a need, without the need there is no motivation to abstain. Even with the need it's hard. But without it, I'd say impossible, at least for a man in his twenties that has had a frequency of multiple times per week.

Mr. L: I am married, so I practice "relative" celibacy. There was a period of celibacy lasting around two years ending three or four months ago that I ended as the relationship with my wife was deteriorating badly. I reverted briefly to a different pattern of a month or so, but recognize such a difference in energy and sensitivity that I am working to longer periods of "relative" celibacy.

Mr. M: Usually a period of celibacy ends because I have given in to a surge of sexual desire. For me the surge of sexual desire that makes celibacy so difficult begins slowly. The real trouble begins when I start (often unknowingly) to make small concessions to the desire. From there the craving rises exponentially in intensity until I give in.

Mr. O: Nature's default took over when I no longer actively decided to be celibate. I decided to be celibate before and during a spiritual retreat. When I returned home, I thought I would keep the celibacy because of the positive effects I had seen, but without a commitment to myself, temptation got the best of me.

Mr. P: Celibacy is not easy. I made a bargain. My side of the bargain was very hard to keep—but I kept it to the best of my capacity—which is to say that I was not always perfect. I was able to be 100% celibate for several years, but still, for 20 years I inhibited my sexual expression to a very high degree. My bargain was that I would yield to nature after I found my answer. Well, the yielding came gradually before the answer came—but I am convinced the practice of inhibition was essential to my eventual success in my spiritual quest. Finally I got married (at age 39) after which celibacy is impractical—though a disciplined life style is still advisable and beneficial.

Knowing when to end a commitment is one of the most difficult decisions to make honestly. We are experts at spinning stories that make us look like reasonable and wise individuals. Celibacy helps us see our story-making in action and hopefully allows us to better know when the discipline has had its utmost effect.

Chapter V
Advice

Negative suggestions to the mind are not very effective. For example, [for someone practicing celibacy] "I will not have sex" is not as workable as "I wish to be free of sex." – Richard Rose in Rose Quotes and Notes: 1986-1993[23]

This chapter contains more advice on celibacy than any other source I'm aware of. Sharing their practical experiences, what advice would our respondents give to someone trying celibacy?

Mr. A: Don't vilify sex or women or men (the apparent objects of your lust). When I saw a beautiful girl, I found the best thing to do was to acknowledge her beauty and allure, tip my hat to it in unashamed honest appreciation, but respectfully decline to follow with eyes or thoughts; I had something more important to do for the time being. Celibacy is a tool. It is made out of nitroglycerine. It is a very good tool for a spiritual seeker. Probably the best tool there is. If it is overused, it will warp the tool user. People abstaining from something often grow to believe that the things that they are avoiding are evil. This can result in their turning in another direction while being prompted by subconscious manifestations of sex-based inner promptings.

Make conscious, out loud, even spoken statements of intention regarding proposed sexual activity. For example: "I will abstain from all sexual activity, physical and mental, for the specific purpose of transmuting whatever quanta of energy there is related to that activity into fuel for the mental and spiritual striving towards (fill in the blank, whatever objective you have in mind).

Don't worry too much about dreams that result in a release of sexual activity. Just don't allow yourself to slyly get too busy in this direction. I found that every few months, there was an automatic pressure release thing that would occur during sleep. I think one has to learn how to accept that some things happen and keep marching on, while at the same time not letting this get too out of hand—the body is very sly; like a misbehaving kid, it will push things until an adult tells them where the limit is.

Remind yourself or just address yourself whenever it seems necessary: "I am practicing celibacy for a purpose. I am doing something with my life that is a maximum purpose. I am serious about this."

Celibacy is not forever. It is for a specific amount of time. That specific amount of time is the time that you are a dedicated, devoted, dynamic seeker of the ultimate reason for your being. When you drop that activity, you can drop celibacy, too, wherever you are standing at the time.

Mr. B: First, celibacy means total abstinence from any type of sexual orgasm. Some people seem to think that if you are not having sexual intercourse, that you can indulge in masturbation and still call it celibacy. Not true. It means total abstinence.

Beware that the only real temptation you will encounter is the temptation that you allow in your own head. I believe that to be celibate, not only must the body come under control, but more importantly, the mind first and foremost, so that indulging in sexual reverie is a reversal and will lead to physical indulgence.

That all reverie seems to come from outside of the inner mind, thus possibly entity induced.

That your former life of sexual indulgence is living under another's thumb, thus you really don't have any free-will or original thoughts while you are living and indulging in sex. Your real function is fertilizer.

As a man, when celibate, women appear to be totally vampire-like when it comes to their function with sex, however the celibate man appears to hold no interest to them. The only ego trip is in your own head and that is part of the nature game to get you functioning again as a sexual "milking machine."

Mr. C: Make your commitment explicit. Write it down. Decide a finite period of time for which you will be celibate. Tell someone else (someone not of the opposite sex) of your commitment, and have them hold you to it. Make part of your commitment be that you will confess any lapses to whomever is helping you hold to your commitment. These are just common-sense, psychological tools to help you in your resolve.

If you can, live in an environment relatively free of the opposite sex. I found celibacy to be effortless when I was in isolation; with no outside stimulus to stir up the desire, the drive eventually subsides and is easily sublimated. If you are surrounded by young bodies and an over-sexualized media (i.e. most college campuses these days) it is almost impossible to be naturally celibate; you might develop self-control, but it is unlikely you will develop peace of mind, especially if you are young.

Have absolute faith that you can wait out any desire. Most lapses in celibacy come from succumbing to the belief that this desire will never go away, that the only way to relieve yourself of this burden is to give into the desire. If you see, with absolute faith and clarity, that the desire will go away if you ignore it, you can be free of it within five minutes.

Jesus was right; if you sin in your heart, it's as bad as if you sin in the act. If you give yourself over to sexual reverie, your celibacy is wasted at best, and almost certainly doomed to fail. Every thought has a certain mental inertia which will inevitably lead you to action if tolerated.

That being said, accept that you are human. You do not need to feel guilty about being a sexual being. You just need to be determined to be more than that.

Mr. D: Mr. Rose often said that after a certain point in celibacy, you can only tempt yourself. I unfortunately also discovered, many times, that this is a very true statement. He used the expression, "…when your power is upon you" to indicate that time when a critical mass had been reached, so to speak, and the person was decidedly "on the Path." Leastwise, I presume, this is what he meant. This same achievement also can bring other side effects, which in the end may well prove to be ego based, or similar to the stone-to-bread meal the devil encouraged Christ to enjoy.

The most difficult hurdle on the road to a celibate lifestyle may be in fact one of the very problems, which a period of celibacy may alleviate, and that is mental confusion. The problem is that a person whose thinking is confused is very likely to reject the idea as absurd or worse, and in this determination, effectively seal themselves into the confused state. I note here that there are no strict specific "requirements" for Enlightenment (Union with the Absolute), but that many noted people, spiritual or otherwise, have remained celibate for at least periods of time, during their productive lives.

Mr. E: Try to be around someone else who has been successful with it, especially if they are currently being celibate, and if you can't get that, be around someone else who is struggling with trying to be celibate, and if not that, try to make yourself accountable with someone who has had relative success at it, because no one else is trying to be celibate, and it will take a lot of extra will power to overcome the doubts you'll have about whether or not this is worth it, without that extra accountability.

Also, try to remove things that are of a sexual nature. I had to delete the pornography from my computer. Or, try to not let your eyes linger on women. Or some billboards. Or some internet advertisements. It seems that way you have less sex-related thoughts throughout the day, and so there's less of an inner conflict later.

When I first started, when it was still rocky, I told myself I was going to focus on only this one commitment to be celibate, and I wasn't going to worry if I had a lousy meditation record or any of that—I just wanted to focus on trying to be celibate. I think that attitude helped because otherwise I might have said to myself, "Well it's ok to go do something that would not be in line with my commitment to be celibate because it will help me meditate" which would not have helped either commitment. When I started, I intended to keep trying until I was being celibate—I didn't plan on trying it and if it failed, give up. This attitude was easier to have because I was getting confrontation on why I wasn't being celibate, so for me, confrontation probably helped a lot.

Mr. G: I remember hearing a priest being interviewed on the radio about the practice of celibacy in the priesthood; he said that "it requires a tremendous level of emotional maturity." I thought that was a good way to say it—how do I live with the "strongest force in the universe" which also happens to be inside me, particularly with the more than suggestive material which is now… everywhere. How to deal with the loneliness, etc. There's a lot to talk about, however the key thing to remember is this joke:

A young priest moves into his new parish. He asks the older outgoing priest, "Father may I have a word with you?"

"Yes, my son, what is it?"

"Father, this woman thing, when does it leave you?"

"Oh, about three hours after you're dead."

Mr. H: I used to have a more puritanical view, that length of time was the only factor, but now I think effort applied over time is a definite factor. Otherwise I can't explain my own recent history. I think too, that the reasons for celibacy are very important. When I was celibate because of fear or guilt, it was not the same as when I abstained because I really believed in it.

I used to think that it would soon be an easy thing to be abstinent, now I'm amazed anyone, including myself, can ever get free for any time at all.

Mr. I: Don't get drunk.

Learn to turn the head away from sexual thinking. Something that might help in this is realizing that you are a pawn of that thinking, and that the promised pleasure is just nature's bait to get those genes passed on.

Another thing that might help in this is seeing the absurdity of the mating game. By recognizing that girls wearing alluring clothing are not only doing it for attention, but are also doing it out of a fundamental questioning of their own self worth, it makes it easier to be objective about the feelings engendered. On top of that, both they and the person trying to be celibate are usually responding to unconscious promptings they receive from their environment and their hormones.

Mr. J: When you get into trouble, and you are tempted, pray thusly: "I wish to be free of ____." For example, "I wish to be free of thoughts about sex." This is a positive, powerful way of turning thoughts away from temptation.

Alcohol, for me, was not a danger, but in the right circumstances a drunken state of mind will remove all inhibitions. Do not consume alcohol when you know it will weaken your resolve.

For men, the body will protect itself (i.e., the prostate) through nocturnal emissions. This is not a conscious engagement in sexual activity and does not constitute a breach of celibacy.

On both the mundane and spiritual levels, you should refrain from thinking that celibacy makes you superior to others.

Work with others in a group who are of similar thinking and engaged in a compatible spiritual path. Though you may not find other celibates, it helps to talk and associate with others who are working on compatible spiritual systems of thinking.

If you are young, start now. In my opinion, practicing celibacy while you are young will have positive effects that will last a lifetime.

When you break the celibacy, you should continue to engage in sexual temperance. In fact, I advise that you remain especially vigilant in refraining from excessive or unusual sexual practices, as "nature" may call on you to repay your debt, perhaps in a harsh way.

Mr. K: Possible avenue to success: find a need for [extra] energy. It can be anything, spiritual or material. Determine that the need can be fulfilled by salvaging energy from the reproductive system. Make a commitment in words that are written. Memorize the commitment. Say it mentally when imagery sets in. I've also "battled" the imagery from settling in. It seems one can either turn the head from the imagery or attack whatever is bringing it in head on. Regardless, the imagery itself must not be looked at.

Possible tests to commitment: I swear women can smell when a man has been celibate for a period of time. I have noticed without fail that when I am celibate women are more interested. This seems to be just another cruel trick devised to test the commitment. I have had the most unbelievable stories happen to me just a day or two after committing to a period of celibacy.

Two tips: 1) Get rid of all pornographic material, this includes the internet. 2) One cannot date and be celibate at the same time, period.

Mr. L: The real science is not only physical but mental. We are bombarded daily by the media, and by fashion. With all these promptings, it is truly a practice that requires turning the mental attention to something else. When the heat is on, get outside and do something physical to exhaust the energy and take the mind away from such thoughts. Rose used to advise people to tell themselves, "Later—I will do something about this later" as a way of getting the mind back to the real problem.

Mr. M: My advice would be to watch for the first sign of sexual craving and fight the battle then instead of later when it has gotten out of control.

Mr. N: Don't assume that a successful period of celibacy, regardless of the duration, means that it's unassailable. During the years of struggling to reestablish celibacy on a firm footing, I had the feeling that it was like playing a chess game with a master who was always three steps ahead of me. I couldn't outwit the seeming adversity. But eventually I found that whenever I honestly felt myself backed into a corner and prayed for help from within, the help was ready, willing, and able to blast the adversity with a power that was unimaginable.

Mr. O: I would recommend to try it out for a period: see for yourself how you are affected and if it is helpful. Pay special attention to what happens when you break the celibacy. This will give you a much better foundation for deciding whether to be celibate or not. Another thing I recommend is to make a written commitment and make it as clear as possible by including the reason, the length of time, etc. If you find it hard to keep the celibacy, a daily reminder of why you are doing it might be helpful (reading the written commitment is one way). When sexual thoughts occur, I find it helpful to turn my attention to awareness watching awareness.

Mr. P: 1) Be persistent, don't give up.
2) Observe the cycle of physical energy and resulting moods and ensuing thoughts that are visited upon you.
3) Prayer.
4) Don't get fat-headed—be watchful of becoming overly narcissistic.

That "the real science is not only physical but mental," sums up this chapter well. Observe the trains of thought that lead to sexual reverie and learn to ignore them by literally turning your interior awareness to another object. As some of the catalysts for these thoughts are external, build a lifestyle that supports your desire. As advertising is saturated with sexual references, reduce your exposure and find friends with something other than sex at the top of their priority list. Make a positive commitment and use the energy you gain for pursuit of your goal.

Though it wasn't mentioned by the survey respondents, one of the best pieces of advice I heard was to realize how a string of bad news or failures can lead domino-like to the breaking of a commitment. An argument, a costly mistake at work or school, a parking ticket—any set of blows may led us to exasperation and frustration; throwing up our hands in despair and throwing our commitment out the window in exchange for the temporary solace of pleasure.

Chapter VI

Message-in-a-Bottle Thoughts

Celibacy was one of the disciplines used to generate additional Mental Quantum, usually with the hope of finding Essence-Realization or GOD. – Richard Rose in Energy Transmutation, Between-ness and Transmission

The final survey question was an open-ended appeal for any other message-in-a-bottle thoughts.

Mr. A: I felt that celibacy was a spiritual necessity for me. I mean, it felt and meant that I was serious and doing something serious with my life. I think when there's nothing ventured, there's nothing gained. Nothing. If you rationalize why you don't need to be celibate, then I say you will fail in whatever grand endeavor you think you are going to try. Try celibacy. Live it. Do it. Then you will have the personal experience to decide whether or not it is still something you should do.

I think that being free from habits that you wouldn't want someone watching you do is maybe freedom for the first time. Like I read in a book called *The Law of Suggestion* by Santanelli (a professional hypnotist's stage name), when I became celibate, I "quit scaring children." I felt pure. I wasn't ashamed and I could walk with my head held high. It was worth it for that alone.

Mr. B: I think the most difficult part for me concerning celibacy has come in retrospect, after having been celibate. Only later did I come to understand better what Rose said "you have to kill the umpire before he kills you."[24] I woke up one day and looked next to me and realized that my thinking had resulted in marriage that began with sex that started with a massive outwitting going on inside my head that "I," the umpire, had allowed to happen.

I believe celibacy for an extended period is a "must" for any spiritual seeker to help clarify your own thinking, define who you are in the body in a more real sense, free yourself from previous sexual associations and habits that are affecting everything from your body health to your personality projection and your innermost thoughts, an opportunity to understand more comprehensively what "living" is, what "thinking" is, and to get an inkling of what "retraversing the projected ray of life" may be all about by actually reversing your former role of dissipating through sex—which is a function of doing nothing more that "fertilizing" till you drop over dead.

Oh, and don't forget love. I think celibacy taught me that love, between the sexes, hardly exists, other than an excuse for sexual expression, however there are those who would argue this point with me.

Beware of very complex forms of mental outwitting. Anger, self pity and loneliness when you finally become celibate are all thoughts that lead ultimately to sex, and again, it is very interesting to attempt to understand how nature/entities are using the umpire/self/your own head to indulge in seemingly harmless thoughts that have at their root an attempt to move the mind towards thinking that will take you away from celibacy.

Mr. D: My best advice to others, then, is to watch your behavior, first your physical behavior, and then your mental behavior. Precede this with a definite verbal commitment, at least to the God within or our deeper Self. Refrain from surges of pride. Allow yourself to become more sensitive, and to rejoice in the achievement of small progress, for the journey from sleep to the Light is long, lonely and arduous. It is best to be thankful for every speck of manna that comes our way. Despair will soon enough set in, without any encouragement from ourselves through self-pity and self-castigation for our slips and failures. It is only important that we remember to rise one time more than we fall, until all things are taken from us, and we stand naked and alone before the Truth.

Mr. E: My initial thought about celibacy had been "who would want to torture themselves like that!?" But dissipation does not seem like the important part of my life it used to be.

Also, I saw this, but some of the people who have been celibate for longer than I have haven't said they saw this: I noticed a specific point where it was like a [switch flipped] and I knew I wasn't going to have a problem any more. I did have a hiccup ten months later, but before that I hadn't gone two weeks without a hiccup.

Mr. H: I still heartily recommend it, as much for the test of oneself and the way it forces one to see what state of mind is really in play day-to-day. I don't think one could ever transcend the animal/sex state of mind without an extended period of celibacy, unless they were damn lucky.

Mr. I: The effort to be celibate is one of the most difficult that I have ever undertaken, and if you have significant trouble at first, do not be surprised. Take the mistakes you make along the way as things to learn from, and pay close attention to the ways in which you deceived yourself so that in the future, you will be able to nip it in the bud. Do not waste time beating yourself up, unless you have to beat yourself up to insure you don't mess up in the same way again.

There is nothing wrong with sex, save that it has a significant cost of resources which might be otherwise profitably redirected. In order to be celibate successfully you must be convinced of the reason you are doing it, and you may continually have to remind yourself of that reason, especially in light of constant temptation.

Mr. J: Without a doubt, celibacy is a powerful way to accelerate a person's spiritual vector. It is a serious endeavor, but so is the drive to know Truth at all costs. In the Transmission Papers, Rose offers a caveat that is especially worthy of consideration: "Celibacy is a science. It can kill you if you are not a skilled master of it."

Mr. K: Good luck, and when knocked down, get up again, and keep fighting the good fight.

Mr. L: It works. It is a key practice to increase energy, intuition, and clarify your mind. It isn't prescriptive, but if you wish to catalyze your actions, give it a try. Ignore the derision that greets the mere mention of the subject from those who have not, and likely will not, tread the path of a seeker. Recognize in the stories of men and women of accomplishment their periods of creativity and accomplishment were accompanied by avoiding dissipation. Your body and mind generate a limited amount of energy. If your goal is to know the self, celibacy conserves the energy needed to address the question.

Mr. M: Sexual reverie and release is addictive. Like any addiction, breaking free from it can clear your mind and emotional state.

Mr. N: Remember why you want to be celibate. Remember your ultimate goal. Remember the deep feeling of want, of something missing, of existential anguish. In order to answer to that want, you need mental clarity and the ability to hold your head on a great internal conflict without flinching. Celibacy may be the most important ingredient in the recipe for gaining mental clarity and fortitude.

Mr. O: If you want to accomplish something great, celibacy might be a tool to help you focus your time and energy on your goal. Give it a try and find out for yourself; don't take other people's word for it.

Mr. P: Celibacy is a powerful tool on a spiritual path. It will reveal yourself to yourself in short order. I know of nothing else that simultaneously affirms and diminishes the sense-of-self in ways that are completely conducive to the path of self-inquiry. Celibacy creates conflict within the mind at the same time that it gives the energy needed to focus the attention to observe that conflict and the consistency of a point-of-observation for observing that conflict along with everything else within one's field of attention. Beyond that, there are side effects of celibacy that are difficult to articulate, let alone prove—except that the proof is there for anyone willing to carry out the experiment. These side-effects include what may be thought of as extra-sensory perception. Considering that all perception is mental in nature—it is a heightened sensitivity of the nervous system and the mental machinery that processes the input that I think enables a "hearing" and a "seeing" that is not limited only to light hitting the eyeballs or sound striking the ear drums. There seems to be a more direct avenue to perception that celibacy facilitates. Rupert Sheldrake the botanist has done research into this—not the celibacy angle, but the mechanism or phenomena of direct mental perception and knowledge.

In my own case I developed a hyper sensitivity that enabled me to literally feel other peoples' physical and emotional states to a point that was actually intrusive. I would literally feel another person's headache, or intoxication on tobacco or pot. I could feel another person's energy level. I could also perceive others' emotions toward me—to the extent that I could perceive their presence and proximity without physically seeing them, and I could sense them at a distance. I corroborated these feeling many times. But the important thing about this is that there seems to be a higher emotional center in us that the sublimation of physical energy activates. I can't elaborate on the details of my experiences with this in this format at this time. I can only say that I was inspired by the experience of what I would call Grace that I believe visited me when most needed—and that I believe surrounds us always—but that we cannot apprehend because our sensibilities are so dulled and buried by the preponderance of gross levels of physical experience that impinges on our consciousness. Celibacy is a break from that.

Chapter VII
To Try and to Fail

Let no one think that it is impossible because it is difficult. It is the highest goal, and it is no wonder that the highest effort should be necessary to attain it. – Mohandas K. Gandhi in The Story of My Experiments with Truth

I have known a few good men who seemingly despite their best efforts never succeeded with long-term celibacy—perhaps a few weeks or days at a time which they compare to the years of others. As Mr. F so painfully states, "This lack of character has caused much sadness for me over the years." This self-judgment caused him to separate from the very people that might have helped him in his struggle.

There are a number of factors at play in this negative spiral. One is comparison to others. All agree that celibacy is highly individualized. I suspect that a person with a high libido may gain as much advantage from a month of celibacy as a less libidinous person does from six months. Years of celibacy for one man may be no greater achievement than a single year for another. We need to relax our desire to compare ourselves to others, observe the benefits we derive from our efforts, and observe the mistakes we make with a determination to avoid similar mistakes in the future.

Two, there is the old feeling that a puritanical God sits in judgment upon our sins. This is so ingrained in the childhood upbringing of some, that even astute philosophic thinkers wrap sex in a haze of wrong-doing and their failures take on the color of moral judgments of their weak character. I recommend a good session of cursing and fist shaking at the heavens, then wait a few minutes for the smiting thunderbolts. They won't come. The only judge resides inside us.

One who sincerely tries will find rewards. As we have seen, those rewards will vary. One who tries, finds rewards, then fails has given a good effort and will have incentive to try again. If the length between failures gradually increases, then this is progress.

One who finds no rewards and fails in their effort, has not tried hard enough. As one respondent states, "In spite of having in my possession Rose's paper [*The Albigen Papers*] listing various rationalizations for putting off the spiritual search, I used those very same rationalizations he listed to avoid a commitment to celibacy."

Chapter VIII
The Woman's Experience

Every woman should marry, but no man. – Benjamin Disraeli

By now, you might have noticed that all my survey participants are males. I assure you that is not by design, rather by the fact that, contrary to most spiritual groups, the groups I gravitated toward have a preponderance of males.

I did have one female respondent. I'll reach to the other end of the alphabet and call her... Ms. Z.

❋

Ms. Z: As a female spiritual seeker I have gained tremendously from periods of celibacy in my quest for truth. I have always been amazed at the clarity, energy, intuition... that occurred even with just 28 days of celibacy. I highly recommend trying it at least for these 28 days, even if just for the health benefits. If no benefits come to you, or if one feels more troubled or physically ill, then stop of course. But do try again every once in a while.

A warning to the wise—if one identifies with being the celibate one you can get a strong ego-personality going. And none of us need any more of these egos mucking up the world.

❋

Mr. Rose was a careful observer of the animal world and noted that the animals were superior to us in some ways. One shared trait, though, was the ovarian clock. Females are only fertile at certain times. Their bodies, and consequently their minds are more receptive to sex at those times. "For this reason, celibacy for females involves a different discipline than for males," he said.[25] He didn't expound on that statement, though.

I never heard Mr. Rose talk about women being celibate, but I did talk with one woman who worked closely with him. "Live the celibate life. It's a beautiful life," is what she was told. He advised watching the menstrual cycle and its effect on one's thinking. "You realize your cycle wants children," though it may take years of study to finally accept this. As with men, Rose's advice differed among women. He advised many women to have children, feeling that was a part of their spiritual path.

Observation of the menstrual cycle reveals that the thoughts are influenced by changes in hormones. One woman found that days 1-5 brought sadness for not having children, and days 12-14 turned her thoughts to finding a sexual partner. On days 21-28 she focused on seeking a spiritual answer.

Awareness of these changing mind states allowed her to use them strategically. Days 1-5 proved the optimal times for intuition to occur naturally. During days 16-19, intuition met logic in perfect balance and optimized thinking over difficult concepts. Days 21-27 were the most logical days; helpful for viewing an issue in terms of cold hard logic with little emotion.

Doubtless, women will vary to the degree their thinking is influenced by their cycle and the correspondence of days to thought patterns. The only way to discover is to observe and record the observations over a period of months. You will then gain valuable insight into your self and the source of your thoughts and desires making endeavors such as celibacy easier.

Chapter IX
In Summary

I undertook this project with the desire to help two groups of people: those currently practicing celibacy and those considering the practice. For the first group, I hope you've found inspiration and practical advice that will help you continue. For the second group, I hope you've seen that celibacy is not the purview solely of monks and nuns, or a spiritual anachronism. Celibacy is an experiment rich in revelations about the mind and body and continues to be a part of the path of life for many people.

Celibacy that springs from a desire to focus one's energy is as natural as tuning out distractions when reading a particularly difficult passage or when deeply engaged in a conversation. Only this time, the conversation is with our self and the object of attention is our interior landscape.

If you are inspired to try celibacy and desire for more advice than you find in this booklet, contact the TAT Foundation at the website Tatfoundation.org. At the least, they can help you find a friend on the path with whom you can discuss your concerns.

References

1 Elizabeth Abbott, *A History of Celibacy* (Da Capo Press, 2001).

2 Richard Rose, *Energy Transmutation, Between-ness and Transmission* (TAT Foundation, 1985), 19.

3 John Kent, "Richard Rose's Psychology of the Observer: The Path to Reality Through the Self" (Ph.D. diss., University for Humanistic Studies, 1990), 472-473.

4 Rose, *Energy Transmutation, Between-ness and Transmission*, 46.

5 Rose, *Energy Transmutation, Between-ness and Transmission*, 42.

6 The Three-Fold Path – working with others, being honest about one's self, and a life of active seeking and practice. See Richard Rose's *The Albigen Papers* for more information on the three-fold path.

7 Stefan Lovgren, "Sex and Sports: Should Athletes Abstain Before Big Events?" February 22, 2006, National Geographic News.

8 MS Exton, "Endocrine response to masturbation-induced orgasm in healthy men following a 3-week sexual abstinence," World Journal of Urology 19, no. 5 (2001):377-82. This study showed that testosterone increased with abstinence.

9 Abbott, 208-212.

10 The Hindu: Sports Digest, March 4, 2002, http://www. hinduonnet.com/2002/03/04/stories/2002030403281900.htm (accessed April 23, 2009).

11 William J. Cromie, "Meditation Changes Temperatures: Mind controls body in extreme experiments," *Harvard University Gazette*, April 18, 2002.

12 *The Shakers: Hands to Work, Hearts to God,* dir. Ken Burns, 1985.

13 Lovgren. Unfortunately, Jannini's study (often referenced to discredit avoiding sex before sports) was of men suffering from erectile dysfunction (though their ED was non-hormone related).

14 *The Amplified New Testament* (Zondervan Publishing House, 17th edition), Luke 18:17, Mark 10:15.   Matthew 18:3 says, "Unless you repent (change) and become like little children you can never enter the kingdom of heaven."

15 Weston Agor, *Intuitive Management* (Prentice-Hall, 1984).

16 Mary Kaiser, et. al., "Development of intuitive theories of motion," Developmental Psychology 22, no. 1 (Jan 1986): 67-71.

17 Richard Rose, *Psychology of the Observer* (TAT Foundation, 2001).

18 Confrontation – a technique advocated by Richard Rose to help develop rapport and clarify one's thinking. Ideally, it involves a Socratic-style questioning which reveals unknown assumptions, rationalizations and inconsistencies in thinking. Without a skilled moderator, it tends to devolve into ego-based debate and defense.

19 Richard Rose, *Meditation,* (Pyramid Press, 1981), 15.

20 Engrams – an association that is psychologically painful. See the work of L. Ron Hubbard.

21 Between-ness – a paradoxical determined/not-caring, or relaxed, intense effort that Rose felt led to magical results. See his *The Direct-Mind Experience* book for more information.

22 Entities – Rose suspected that the energy generated during sex was used by unseen beings. These beings have some ability

to manipulate humans into dissipating their sexual energy. A parallel thought was expressed in the film *The Matrix* in which the energy of humans was used to power a world of machines.

23 Richard Rose Quotes and Notes, 1986 to 1993, Part 3: Sexual Lifestyle, http://www.searchwithin.org/download.htm (accessed May 21, 2009).

24 Umpire – the aspect of the mind which is chiefly concerned with survival of the body and species. One can become aware of and observe its functioning. See Rose's *Psychology of the Observer* book for more information.

25 Rose, *Energy Transmutation, Between-ness and Transmission*, 48.

About TAT

Richard Rose created the TAT Foundation in 1973 in order to encourage people who were searching for an answer to their deepest life-questions to work together. TAT members, both those who knew Richard Rose personally and newcomers, are continuing those efforts more than thirty-five years later. We're a community of seekers and finders with four gatherings each year. Individual members sponsor local self-inquiry groups in their areas as well as online groups.

Please visit www.tatfoundation.org for more information on our activities.

LaVergne, TN USA
13 October 2009
160697LV00005B/1/P